I0153439

PARENTS, PLEASE!
STOP SPANKING YOUR CHILDREN

PHYSICAL DISCIPLINE ISN'T THE BEST WAY

AN EASY-TO-FOLLOW WORKBOOK
TO HELP YOU STOP SPANKING

PARENTS, PLEASE!
STOP SPANKING YOUR CHILDREN

PHYSICAL DISCIPLINE ISN'T THE BEST WAY

AN EASY-TO-FOLLOW WORKBOOK
TO HELP YOU STOP SPANKING

JULIE ROBINSON, PSYD, LMFT, M.ED.

Halo
PUBLISHING
INTERNATIONAL

Photo credit: Glenn Grayson

Halo
PUBLISHING
INTERNATIONAL

Halo Publishing International
7550 W IH-10 #800, PMB 2069,
San Antonio, TX 78229

First Edition, October 2024
ISBN: 978-1-63765-661-7
Library of Congress Control Number: 2024915048

This book is dedicated to my husband, Richard, and my sons, Brandon and Logan. You inspire me every day to be my best self. I am forever grateful to you all for loving me unconditionally.

CONTENTS

PREFACE

Thank you for listening to the small voice within you that urged you to pick up this book. We all know instinctively that using any type of physical means to get our children to comply is not the best way. And yet we continue the unhealthy practices that were used on us in the name of doing "what was best" for us. This book was not written to shame you or make you feel bad. Everyone can lose their temper, be frustrated and overwhelmed, and react in ways that are not intended. And that is exactly why I have written this book: to help you react in ways that you *do* intend, that do not do long-term damage to your child.

Do you think spanking your child is necessary to help them learn and become a good human being? If you answered yes, I urge you to read this book. Not only is it unnecessary, but it is also counterproductive to helping them become healthy, happy, and effectively functioning human beings.

What is your job as a parent? To discipline and show your children how the world is, to get them to comply no matter what? I would like you to consider reframing your perspective of parenting and to change it from disciplining to teaching. As a therapist, I hear parents share that sometimes spanking is necessary. If you feel you need to physically hit your child—spank, swat, or slap, however you describe it—that shows you have lost control of your emotional state, and you need to remove yourself from the situation and cool down. One job we have as a parent or caregiver is to model and teach positive ways to process frustration. When you spank your child, you show them the opposite, and actions speak louder than words.

My parents were amazing, and they helped me become who I am today. Both my mother and father showered me with love and supported what I wanted for myself; their impact on my life is priceless.

Also true is that my dad had a temper, and when my hyperactivity drove him to a breaking point, he spanked me; one time, I remember, my behind bled around his handprint. Did this help me to stop being hyper? No, it did not. What it did do was cause me to be hypervigilant, to develop a hypersensitive scare response and a lifelong anxiety that something I may do, even unknowingly, could cause me to be hit, and I don't want that.

Spanking and other physical means of discipline, including verbal and emotional abuse, leave scars that last a lifetime. It isn't that I am unable to live my life. I am; I just also live with these traits that can make life more difficult than it needs to be. If you can stop spanking your child today, they won't have to endure any more scars from you; I am sure inflicting permanent damage is not what you ever intend to do.

Again, my intention is not to shame anyone with this book. My dad was the best, and I love him very much. I feel compelled to share this information to help you stop this toxic strategy and begin to parent consciously, loving your child and yourself unconditionally. If your response is that you do love your child unconditionally, I would say we do not hit people we love.

Moving your definition of parenting from disciplining your child to teaching them is key. This shift from punishment to support will improve not only your life, but also your relationship with your children. I know you are stressed and doing your best with the information you have. Now, you have more information and can make different, healthier choices to assist you in helping your child learn to identify, give voice to, and manage their emotions. That, instead of inflicting punishment, is our primary job as parents.

Your child is learning; we are all learning. Human beings learn more effectively in loving, supportive environments. You can take the Spank No More pledge and learn new ways to interact with your children, which will lead to more positive behaviors and interactions.

Thank you for taking the time to ensure that you really do not have to hit your children to teach them. I promise you, you don't!

INTRODUCTION:

THE OUTDATED PRACTICE OF PHYSICAL DISCIPLINE

Physical discipline has been embedded and normalized within our cultural fabric for far too long. Parenting manuals of the past, popular sayings, movies, television shows, and even some modern societal norms have perpetuated the idea that spanking is an effective way to manage children's behavior. However, the objective of this book is to show you why this isn't true and to help you find a new way. This book delves into the negative effects of physical discipline on children's physical and mental well-being, including its harmful impact on their self-esteem, their trust in their parents, and their ability to form healthy relationships in the future. The book also highlights alternative methods of teaching that are more effective in promoting positive behavior in children, such as positive reinforcement, communication, unconditional love, and setting clear boundaries.

Ultimately, this book aims to give parents and caregivers the knowledge and tools they need to raise well-adjusted and emotionally healthy children without physically disciplining them. I encourage you to consider new ways to discipline and teach your child.

We need to start a different conversation about discipline. One that understands a child's need for guidance instead of focusing on punishment, and one that recognizes the long-lasting harm that physical discipline can cause. Through this book, I intend to promote understanding of the detrimental effects of spanking and to provide concrete, effective alternatives to physical discipline. We will explore the psychology of children, how they understand the world, and how their minds interpret spanking. We will take a hard look at the emotional trauma often associated with physical discipline and its potential to turn into a spiral of violence.

Another aim of this book is to empower parents with practical and respectful alternatives to physical disciplining, and to suggest a kinder approach to teaching children to extinguish unwanted behaviors. Some of these methods include positive language, chill-outs, mutual respect, and, perhaps most importantly, unconditional love. We will explore these techniques in depth and gain an understanding of why they work and how to apply them.

Real-life examples of families successfully transitioning from physical discipline to these alternatives will be provided. Their stories will serve as inspiration and proof that raising well-behaved, respectful children is possible without spanking. I will also discuss therapists' crucial role in supporting families throughout this process. Often, the act of spanking is a learned behavior passed down from generation to generation. Unlearning these patterns requires hard work, commitment, and often professional guidance.

In the concluding chapters, we will examine strategies to break the cycle of physical discipline and move toward raising emotionally healthy children. This book is a comprehensive guide for any parent or caregiver who wants to understand and improve their methods of interacting with children. Further, this book isn't just about stopping spanking; it's about a paradigm shift in how we view discipline and its role in parenting.

I recommend we reframe how we define parenting and what we believe is helping children to thrive. It's about treating our children with the same respect and kindness we wish to teach them to show others. This is also about breaking cycles and making life better for each child and family.

There is no time to waste; it starts here and now. Let's begin this journey to explore why you should stop spanking your children and start discovering the healthier, more effective ways that can take its place. The next spank, slap, punch, or harsh language you impose on a child could be the moment that completely breaks their trust in you. Now is the time to make this change.

TAKE THE PLEDGE

NO-MORE-SPANKING DAY

This is an exciting day because it is the last day you need to use any form of physical discipline with your child. It doesn't feel good to you when you do it; you can feel instinctively that it isn't the best option, so today is the day to stop this toxic strategy. This book has been written to provide an alternative to how you currently interact with and view your child or children. To allow you to be the most effective parent you can be, I am asking you to examine your parenting lens and clear away any bias you discover.

I have also raised kids and understand how challenging it can be. You work hard, but you are tired; you try to be the best parent you can be with what energy you have. Sometimes the kids act up while you are feeling overwhelmed, and your instinct is to spank, swat, or hit them in some fashion to get their attention, no matter what. This book will help you realize there are many other effective ways to gain their compliance without spanking or other physical means of coercion.

Starting today, you can promise yourself, and your kids, that you will find another way, no matter what. They can depend on you to be loving and to maintain some degree of patience in all interactions, no matter how tired you are. If you can at this point say out loud, in front of other people, "I think spanking or using physical means of multiple types is the best option in some situations to help my child learn," I urge you to please read the book and then see how you feel. The intention here is to help you find healthy, supportive strategies that will support you in teaching your child, lead to better outcomes, and build a stronger relationship between the two of you. The scientifically proven, long-term emotional and physical damage caused by physical means of discipline and coercion isn't easily healed. It is important to remember that the lasting negative effects are often carried into adulthood.

Please consider taking this pledge now and commit yourself to reading this book with the intention of following the suggestions wholeheartedly. Don't you and your child deserve a better way?

I, ____________________________, commit today to not using physical means of any kind with my child from this point forward. Also, I intend to engage in the strategies offered to see if they work. Whether it is for discipline or teaching, I promise not to hit, spank, swat, or in any way use my hands or any other object on my child or children. I will choose another option of some sort; this is a line I will no longer cross.

Signature(s)

________________________ ________________________

Date

____

CHAPTER 1

REASSESS: IS SPANKING REALLY BEST?

The data on whether spanking and other physical means of discipline inflict lasting harm is in. It does.

The effects of spanking has been a topic of interest for many years. Numerous studies suggest spanking can have negative consequences for children. For example, Gershoff (2002) found a consistent association between corporal punishment (including spanking) and negative outcomes for the child. The study concluded that "corporal punishment is associated with an increased risk of aggressive behavior, delinquency, and mental health problems in children." Also, Grogan-Kaylor (2005) completed a longitudinal study that examined the relationship over time between corporal punishment and antisocial behavior. The findings suggested that "children who experienced corporal punishment were more likely to exhibit increased antisocial behavior as they grew older."

In addition, Afifi et al. (2012) "found a significant association between physical punishment (including spanking) and mental health disorders in adults." The research indicated that individuals who were physically punished as children had a higher risk of developing mental health issues later in life. A cohort study by MacKenzie et al. (2012) adds to this. It followed children and found that "exposure to corporal punishment in the first three years of life was associated with lower cognitive scores and more aggressive behavior at age five." And there is a lot more.

Sometimes, when I talk with parents in a session, and they reveal that they have used spanking at times, I ask them if they think it works. They will typically share that it does not stop the unwanted behaviors, which still occur, and they still need to spank occasionally to "get their point across." I then ask, "What is your point? To just get the child to comply, or to teach them and help them to understand? Or to just get them to stop whatever they are doing at the moment, and the slap or spank is just to get their attention?"

I assure you that you are getting their attention. Unfortunately, you are also getting the attention of their autonomic nervous system. This component of the peripheral nervous system regulates involuntary physiologic processes such as heart rate, blood pressure, respiration, and digestion.

So physical discipline can result in a child becoming hypervigilant, jumpy, and easily startled, which is anxiety that can continue throughout their lives. The underlying feeling that you could be hit if you do something wrong—and you frequently find yourself doing something wrong without even knowing it—can be very unsettling emotionally. If you then see the child acting out and not wanting to engage, and punish them further, you are deepening the injury and driving a wedge between you that won't be easy to fix.

In my role as a licensed marriage and family therapist (LMFT), I've witnessed firsthand the negative consequences of physical discipline. I've sat in my office with numerous adults who carry the emotional scars from their childhood spankings. And I can relate because I myself was spanked. I've seen how it can negatively affect relationships, self-esteem, physical health, and mental health. And I've seen parents stuck in a cycle, spanking their own children because it's the only method they know to handle their child's negative behaviors.

If spanking were the answer, it would work after a time or two, or ten, and you wouldn't need to use it indefinitely. The fact that it needs to be done repeatedly with increasing force—and over time, potentially requiring the use of items to inflict punishment, like belts, sticks, shoes, and the like—shows corporal punishment isn't the answer.

ACTIVITY: RECALLING YOUR CHILDHOOD

Write down what types of punishment were imposed on you as a child. Were you spanked? Hit with a belt? Think for a moment, and write down what you can remember.

____

____

____

____

____

Do you feel that spanking helped you feel good about yourself or resulted in your becoming a good person?

____

____

____

Did you ever receive an injury from being spanked—for example, a bruise, welt, or cut resulting in bleeding?

____

____

____

Were you threatened with being hit in an attempt to make you stop a behavior?

____

____

____

Did you see your siblings being punished?

____

____

____

THINGS TO CONSIDER

- There are other ways—besides spanking and other means of physical discipline—to stop unwanted behaviors.
- The evidence is overwhelming that spanking has numerous long-term, negative effects.
- How you respond to a situation is something you *can* control.

If there are better ways—and there are—why would you want to continue spanking or using any type of physical discipline?

You are the one who can change this.
Now is the time to do it.

NOTES AND THOUGHTS

CHAPTER 2

EMOTIONAL TRAUMA: SPANKING'S UNSEEN IMPACT

Children learn from their environment. Each interaction, each moment is an opportunity for learning. When a child is spanked, they aren't simply learning that their behavior is unwanted, they are also learning that physical violence is an acceptable way of expressing dissatisfaction or exerting control. The child may momentarily stop the unwanted behavior, not because they understand the implications, but because they fear the pain and humiliation of spanking. *This forms a negative association with the learning process.*

Spanking, by definition, is a physical act—usually a slap on the child's backside or hand—intended to induce temporary pain and discourage unwanted behavior. While the immediate aim is to eliminate unwanted behavior, research and child psychology show that the real impact is *more profound and damaging*. Spanking can negatively impact a child's emotional health. Children, particularly when they are very young, cannot distinguish which is bad—the act itself or they themselves. So when a parent spanks, a child often interprets it as they are bad, which leads to feelings of shame, sadness, and low self-esteem. This skewed self-perception can follow them into adulthood and affect their relationships, academic performance, and overall mental health.

Spanking models aggressive behavior. A child who is spanked is more likely to resolve their conflicts or express their anger through physical aggression. This inclination isn't confined to their childhood years but could potentially result in a pattern of aggressive behavior in their adult life, impacting their personal and professional relationships.

Trust is the foundation of the parent-child relationship. When a parent or caregiver—the child's primary source of love and protection—resorts to physical pain to discipline, it confuses and frightens the child, breaking that trust. Over time, this rupture can cause the child to withhold their feelings or experiences from their parents for fear of punishment, driving a deep wedge in the relationship.

Numerous studies have associated spanking with an increased risk of mental health disorders, including depression, anxiety, and substance abuse. For example, the study by Lansford et al. (2012) found that "the frequency of spanking, regardless of its form, was associated with an increase in children's anxiety and depression symptoms." The researchers distinguished between spanking and physical abuse, emphasizing that even milder forms of spanking were linked to negative behavioral outcomes in children.

The study shows that spanking can have different effects on children's behavior, and it's important to consider the kind of discipline used. In addition, spanking can create a chaotic family environment and increase the child's exposure to chronic stress. Over time, this stress can lead to significant physical and mental health issues.

Understanding these proven negative effects of spanking is the first step in acknowledging the need for change. It's not about blaming parents who have spanked their children; we are products of our cultural and personal upbringing, after all. But it's about providing the knowledge and tools necessary to break the cycle and adopt healthier, more effective discipline strategies, which we'll explore in the upcoming chapters.

Remember, it's not about perfection but about striving for progress and understanding. It's about reshaping our disciplinary methods to teach our children in a safe, loving environment, fostering their emotional, cognitive, and social growth. And, most importantly, it is about ensuring that our children perceive discipline as a learning experience, not a fear-inducing punishment.

ACTIVITY: TRAUMATIC FEELINGS

Write down feelings you remember about physical punishments you've received.

____

____

____

____

____

Do you experience anxiety?_______________________

____

Do you experience symptoms of depression?_____________

____

Are there feelings you still remember and think about at times when remembering being spanked or physically disciplined?__________

____

____

THINGS TO CONSIDER

- Spanking and other types of physical discipline cause emotional trauma.
- Anxiety and depression can start while your child is young and continue into adulthood.
- Your child's trust is not easy to rebuild.

The emotional scars from spanking and other types of physical discipline last throughout a person's lifetime.

You are the one who can change this.
Now is the time to do it.

NOTES AND THOUGHTS

CHAPTER 3

PARENTING REDEFINED: FROM DISCIPLINE TO TEACHING

This change to no longer spank requires you to shift your thinking, which, in turn, requires that you change how you view your role as a parent or caretaker. Please open your mind to consider this perspective—being a parent is a gift and a responsibility.

Being a parent or caregiver means that another human being is dependent on you for their every need. This starts the moment they are born and continues as the young child models all that you do and say and depends on you to support them in discovering who they are and what they love as an adolescent and young adult. If your primary focus is the child getting to know and understand what you love and engaging solely in things you enjoy, you are missing out on the opportunity to find out what lights them up and what they are drawn to. *And it is this process that allows an individual to understand their passion and purpose.* This is the time!

When your focus is on teaching, you are looking at your child and the situation through a different lens. You are not focusing on pointing out what is wrong or missing or what you are not happy with. You are instead focused on what type of support your child may need to be successful in whatever they are doing. This could be simply walking into your child's room and seeing them playing with a toy in a way that doesn't seem correct to you. For example, they could be driving a plane on the ground or flying a car, and you step in to show them the correct way the car or plane moves. This little correction can extinguish the child's intrinsic motivation and creativity and cause them to feel that they don't know how to do things correctly and don't know how to fix themselves. Ultimately, these feelings can lead to learned helplessness (Peterson et al., 1993), and they will stop trying because they feel their efforts will never be enough.

Or you could see a child using a chair to get something off the counter and yell at them or yank them down out of frustration. Using the five-step process presented in a later chapter, you can switch from disciplining to teaching. Explain why you don't want them to use the chair in that way—they could get hurt. Your primary concern is safety; therefore, explaining that in terms the child can understand is the aim here. Yelling and saying, "I have told you a million times not to climb on the chair," can escalate to grabbing them by the arm to get their attention. This teaches them that it is okay to grab someone to get their attention. It doesn't teach them that when they make a mistake, they have an opportunity to learn and try again. And then, when they grab someone at school to get their attention, they will get in trouble.

Physical discipline can be a harmful cycle that gets passed down from one generation to the next. Many people believe that spanking is necessary for a good parent, but this is a misconception. Often, parents who use physical discipline were themselves disciplined physically as children. It's not just a disciplinary method, but a pattern that's deeply rooted in family culture and society as a whole.

Your job as a parent is to love your child unconditionally—truly without conditions—and to support them in knowing and reaching for their dreams. Your job isn't to try to shape them into something you want them to be. *They need your support and help to recognize what they want for themselves.* They are not less than anyone; they do not have an unimportant perspective just because they are children. They are wise and should be allowed to talk and be listened to.

Parents, not children, should be responsible for housework and meals. I've heard parents explain that they provide a nice home, food, and clothing, and that is all they feel they are *required* to do. This is also a misconception. Even if that was your experience while growing up, you don't have to model your parents' behavior. Children need unconditional love and unconditional support.

If you are stressed-out and heightened emotionally, that is the time to give yourself a break and not escalate the situation. I'm not saying kids don't benefit from contributing to the household; however, too many chores can cause them to feel stress and anxiety that will negatively affect their schoolwork and mood. Children need time to think and be curious about things. It is not necessary to try to fill every waking moment of their time. Let them have time to discover what interests them and to dream about their future. They need time to rest and play. It isn't laziness; it is important to their development. Kids are just as exhausted as their parents; they need time away from school and homework to *just be*.

Parentification is when a child is required to perform duties that are normally performed by a parent, for whatever reason, including taking care of siblings, the parents, or the home. There are multiple studies showing the negative effects of parentification; one is Chase (1999), which discusses the "negative effects on children's emotional and psychological development." Another is by Greenburg and Jurkovic (1999), which explores the "impact of the loss of childhood experiences, including the emotional toll it takes on children."

Unfortunately, it doesn't take much thought to create human life, which can lead to individuals having children when they never intended to or were not ready. But now that you have them, it is your responsibility to provide them with the best upbringing you can. You can choose to think about things in new ways that enable you to see alternatives to corporal punishment.

ACTIVITY: NEW WAYS OF THINKING

Read the following table to see more supportive ways to reframe how you are explaining what is happening. How you perceive it determines how you react.

Discipline	Teaching
Spanking for not doing chores on time.	Finding out why they are having trouble and helping them find solutions.
Spanking for talking back.	Asking why they responded that way and explaining how it makes you feel.
Spanking for getting bad grades.	Talking with them to find out what they are struggling with and providing support. Let them know that grades are only one indicator of learning.
Spanking for not listening.	Letting your child know that you want their full attention to tell them something important.
Yelling when you first come home from work that nothing is done.	Show them you love them by greeting them as you would someone you care about.
Being angry at your child for relaxing or playing games and calling them lazy.	Helping them to learn balance and being happy that they have found something they enjoy and can be good at.

THINGS TO CONSIDER

- Change your definition of parenting from disciplining to teaching.
- Discipline is a form of control based on fear; teaching is designed to instruct based on love and acceptance.
- You are in control of how you explain things to yourself; there are multiple truthful explanations for anything that is happening.

The emotional scars from spanking and other types of physical discipline last throughout a person's lifetime and can lead to unnecessary symptoms of anxiety and depression.

You are the one who can change this.
Now is the time to do it.

NOTES AND THOUGHTS

CHAPTER 4

FOCUS ON YOU: REGAINING CONTROL OF YOUR EMOTIONAL STATE

How you explain what is happening in every moment is within your control. When your emotions are out of control, it can cause you to overreact and feel as if your responses weren't within your control, but they are. Your emotional reactions are based on what you interpret is happening in any given moment. In the moment you are making the interpretation, if you consciously give yourself time to pause and breathe, this small action will help you begin to regain control over your emotions and your reactions. Spanking or physical discipline often occurs when a parent or caretaker has lost control of their emotions and resorts to physical means out of frustration. Due to your heightened emotional state, you perceive that this extreme reaction is necessary, but it isn't.

Buchanan and Seligman (1995) describe explanatory style as "a cognitive personality variable that reflects how people habitually explain the causes of events to themselves," how they interpret what is happening in any given moment. You attribute a cause to something and explain it that way; however, there is always more than one truthful way to explain what is happening.

For example, when you come home, and the kids are playing in a big mess in the middle of the floor, after you had already texted them that they needed to have everything cleaned up by the time you got there, you could lose your cool. However, regardless of how you are explaining the situation to yourself, when you get home, it is still within your control to choose a more supportive, still-truthful explanation that doesn't set you off. For example, they were having a great time and got carried away.

When you automatically explain to yourself what is happening in any situation, you are not allowing for an accurate interpretation of what is *actually happening*. Automatic responses typically contain unconscious or conscious biases that skew our lens and prevent us from viewing the situation accurately. This can cause us to misinterpret and make inaccurate assumptions. With your conscious awareness—which means to be fully present in this moment and cognizant that what you do and say, as well as what you are thinking, is all under your control—you are responsible for being aware of what is really happening and for not imposing your own misinterpretations on others unconsciously.

How you explain what is happening without receiving any additional information than what you see is based on your *experience, current physical state,* and *current state of mind*. Your past experiences, too, can cause you to be biased that a negative outcome will happen again. Mindfulness strategies such as deep breathing, counting backward from five to one, noticing things around you with your senses to ground yourself, and progressive relaxation can all help to decrease your reactions. More of these resources are listed in Appendix A at the back of the book.

Another thing that can prevent you from being able to respond as you would like is past trauma. You can experience traumatic triggers that are based on negative past experiences you've had that cause you to overreact in this moment. Our brains are amazing; however, they do not know what time it is or if something is actually happening now, or if you are just remembering something or imagining. That is how we are triggered, and our response carries with it all our heightened feelings about past situations.

Using a strategy I call *radical awareness*, you can become more consciously aware in a given moment to allow yourself to see a situation more clearly, consciously stopping your own reaction and changing it. You may feel that it is impossible to stop your reaction, but it is not; with practice, it will become more natural and take less effort. Becoming radically aware allows you to stop the automatic reaction. Once you've stopped that negative momentum, you will see the situation differently and be able to begin to respond in new ways.

If you feel yourself becoming heightened emotionally, that is your cue to take a break and not interact with your child at that time. You could be stressed from work, the drive home, shopping, bills, or a million things that all get focused on your child when you get home. They could just be sitting on the couch, looking at their phone, and you could yell and call them names, tell them they're lazy, or even curse at them. From their perspective, you are unpredictable, and your love is conditional; they are not safe with you.

Some ways that you can practice this are to pause and take a breath before reacting in any way when you feel yourself getting upset. If you are driving home from work, give yourself time to sit in your car before going into the house, time to be in a balanced mental and emotional state when interacting with your child. Listen to music, sing, yell, and get out the energy of the day so that you can be your more relaxed, authentic self with them. You do not have to go over and over all the things you might have said throughout the day that someone could have misinterpreted. It's over; let it go. Don't let the negative events of the day interfere with your relationship with your child and family.

It will be helpful to remind yourself that you will definitely have to tell your child repeatedly—sometimes it feels like endlessly—to do something, *and that is how it is.* There isn't a limit to how many times it takes for them to learn. They will need as much time and as many gentle reminders as they need; that is your job as the parent. I know you are tired. I'm sure you are exhausted, and you work hard. That affects your ability to be present in the moment, which results in being caught up in your own feelings and not being able to control your reaction to your children. You are human, and you, too, are learning and deserve another chance.

For you, this may be a new way of being with your kids, so give yourself time to practice. The same patience and love I'm asking you to show to your children, I'd also like you to show it to yourself as you move through this process. Using radical awareness—becoming radically aware in the present moment—you can see more clearly what is happening without bringing in other outside frustrations.

This is a gift you can give yourself and your child. Put your phone in your pocket and your day filled with issues out of your mind for the moment, and be fully present in greeting your children with love. You deserve it, and so do they. This is a great time to set the tone, bring good energy into your home, and help create a loving environment that supports healthy communication and connection. Your focus on this will prove beneficial.

ACTIVITY: CHANGE YOUR PERSPECTIVE

Read the following table for some more supportive ways to reframe how you are explaining what is happening.

Negative/Pessimistic Explanation	**Positive/Optimistic Explanation**
My child is ignoring me.	My child is focused on something else and doesn't hear me.
My child is being rude to me.	My child is having feelings about something that is affecting how they are able to communicate with me right now.
I need to react immediately and strongly to get my point across.	I need to stop, breathe, and ask what is happening before reacting.
If I don't spank them, they won't listen.	If I take time to be patient with them they will better hear me.
I have to show that I am the boss, or they will run all over me.	If I treat them with respect, they will treat me with respect.
They need to do what I say or else.	I need to be patient with them and help them to learn.
Children need tough love to learn.	Children need unconditional love to learn.
Children are to be seen and not heard; they need to know their place.	Due to their lack of bias, children have insights that adults can benefit from.

THINGS TO CONSIDER

- How you are explaining what is happening in any situation is within your control.
- Past experience can cause us to expect the negative behavior before it happens.
- Considering other truthful explanations is within your power and how you can change your reactions.

How you are explaining what is happening causes you to feel a certain way, which fuels your actions.

You are the one who can change this.
Now is the time to do it.

NOTES AND THOUGHTS

CHAPTER 5

BREAKING THE CYCLE: UNLEARNING YOUR UPBRINGING

From birth to seven years of age, we soak up as fact our parents' and caregivers' explanations for what is happening in this new world around us. So as we get older, we may have never consciously thought about those things or consider with our own thinking mind whether they are actually true for us.

Dr. Bruce Lipton (2015) is a great resource on this topic; he calls it our subconscious programming. And the good news is, these programs can be unlearned with your conscious awareness.

A schema is defined as a cognitive structure that represents a person's knowledge. It is similar to a little box in your mind, into which you put all of your definitions, feelings, and unspoken expectations about a topic or thing. Schemas are built through experience, and from birth to seven years old, we soak up the schemas of our parents or caregivers. A heuristic is a shortcut we've created in our thinking to help us process and organize more quickly the information within the schemas. Both schemas and heuristics are the building blocks for our explanatory style. *These preconceived notions are what are quickly used to help us explain what is happening in every situation.*

For example, in your schema or box for what it means to be a parent, you could believe that a good parent doesn't coddle their child because the lack of coddling makes them strong, or that tough love is necessary to be a good parent, or that you need to spank your child to get them to learn. These are all examples of pessimistic ways of explaining things. Using radical awareness, we can change the way we explain what is happening.

The problem with schemas and heuristics is that they are based on our cognitive distortions, typically in our subconscious, and warped ways of thinking based on our own negative experiences. Without conscious awareness, you can make incorrect snap decisions a million times throughout your day, which can lead to misunderstandings, miscommunication, and hurt feelings.

Research by Sutherland et al. (2019) examined how parents' levels of depressive symptoms affect their children's explanations about the causes of life events. Their findings showed "a significant worsening of the child's explanations due to their parents' depressive symptoms," and the authors recommended teaching the children strategies for examining the accuracy of their thinking.

All of us, most likely, have a few items in various schemas and heuristics that we use daily, but they may no longer align with our true feelings or beliefs. We use these outdated responses in quick decisions, which can lead to miscommunications and misunderstandings.

I hear some parents say, "I was spanked, and I turned out okay." First, that is a subjective, narrowly defined idea. Second, why would you want your children to have to go through something bad unnecessarily? Why do we try to justify, marginalize, and normalize this behavior? It is almost as if we feel we have to defend it; otherwise, our parents could be perceived as bad people. Our parents did what was socially suggested and accepted at the time; they didn't know better. However, we do know better now and must do better for everyone's sake—as individuals, as families, and as a society.

ACTIVITY: CLEAR YOUR LENS

Write down your immediate reactions to the following statements and whether you think they are true or false.

Kids who daydream or engage in fantasy play are lazy and unfocused.

If you are not always doing something, you are being lazy.

A good parent doesn't let their kids talk back to them and will discipline them whenever and wherever it happens, even in front of others or strangers.

If my child disagrees with me, they are defiant and need discipline.

I am the parent, and it is my way or the highway.

While you are living under my roof, you will follow my rules.

I brought you into this world. I can take you out.

Children are not equal to adults and should not be treated as valuable.

No one can tell me what is best for my kids.

THINGS TO CONSIDER

- How you were raised isn't automatically best for your children.
- You may feel that you turned out okay, but that does not mean physical discipline is helpful.
- You can rethink these things now and come to new conclusions based on new information.

How we grew up may have worked for us in some respects; however, parenting your own children in a way that helps them be their best takes your conscious thought and consideration.

You are the one who can change this.
Now is the time to do it.

NOTES AND THOUGHTS

CHAPTER 6

POSITIVE LANGUAGE: UNCONDITIONAL LOVE

Words are powerful; when a tired parent and an unreasonable child mix, it can lead to words that were not intended, that hurt the other, and that damage their bond. Positive language in parenting involves using constructive, encouraging, and affirming words or phrases when communicating with your child. It's about focusing on what *can* be done rather than on what *shouldn't*, fostering a supportive and nurturing learning environment. This ties in with your explanatory style when describing what is happening, especially when in a situation where it is more difficult to use positive language. If your mindset is that your role as a parent is to teach, then it is easier to access that type of language that is based on unconditional love and the intention to teach, not punish.

Positive language in parenting has several benefits. One benefit is enhanced communication. Using positive language helps children understand expectations clearly without feeling criticized or discouraged. For example, saying, "Great effort! You almost finished your homework...just a little more to go," instead of "You didn't finish your homework," encourages progress. The first approach fosters intrinsic motivation, and the second approach extinguishes it.

Another benefit is boosting your child's self-esteem. When parents use positive and affirming words, children feel valued and capable. Phrases like "You did a great job with that drawing" or "I'm proud of how you handled that situation" can reinforce their confidence, which reinforces their self-esteem, the belief that they are capable.

Using positive language will also help build a positive relationship that involves unconditional love between you and your child. Positive language fosters a nurturing environment and strengthens the parent-child bond. It helps create trust and a sense of security, making it easier for kids to communicate and share their thoughts and feelings.

Rosyada and Retnomurti (2017) describe positive language as "the basic right of children." It is "the most important thing to build their characters" and is "required from their closest environment, family."

In practice, using positive language involves framing instructions positively. Instead of saying, "Stop making a mess," say, "Let's keep our things tidy." You will also benefit from offering encouragement, acknowledging effort and progress, and saying things similar to "You're doing great" or "I believe in you."

Another way positive language is practiced is in active listening. Using positive language involves not just what you say, but how you listen and respond. Being attentive and supportive helps in effective communication. When you are frustrated, this can be more difficult. However, it is critical to slow down and become consciously aware during interactions with your child. Ultimately, positive language is a powerful tool that shapes children's perception of themselves, their capabilities, and their relationship with their parents. It creates an atmosphere of encouragement and support, fostering healthy emotional development in children.

This will not only benefit your interactions with your child. Once you recognize the power of the words you are using in that relationship, you may find you want to adjust the words you are using with your spouse, family, work peers, and even strangers. Positive language leads to more positive interactions every time; it is an expression of unconditional love in action. Use it in your self-talk as well.

ACTIVITY: UNCONDITIONAL LOVE

Some of you may not feel as if you've ever received or given unconditional love. Imagine sending yourself and your child or partner unconditional love as you read through the following scenarios:

- Seeing your kids on their phones late at night
- Being spoken back to
- Seeing your child playing video games when you come home from work
- Seeing your partner on their phone
- Finding dirty clothes on the floor
- Perceiving that everyone stops talking when you enter a room
- Finding dirty dishes in the sink
- Finding laundry still sitting in the washer or dryer
- Finding food in bedrooms
- Sitting in heavy traffic
- Finding a vape pen in your teen's room
- Hearing your child or partner sigh heavily or roll their eyes

Take a moment to reflect on ways you feel you would benefit from unconditional love.

____

____

____

____

____

____

THINGS TO CONSIDER

- Become conscious about how specific words can help you express unconditional love more clearly.
- It is easier to give unconditional love to others if you can give it to yourself.
- This is a new way of being which takes time and patience. Give those to your child, and yourself, as you practice feeling and sharing unconditional love.

As you are reading this, you may recognize that you are unable to think of any relationship in your childhood and beyond when you felt authentic unconditional love. Love that wasn't based on any conditions at all. You can change this pattern and give it to your child, to others, and to yourself. How it makes your heart and physical body feel is life-changing.

You are the one who can change.
Now is the time to do it.

NOTES AND THOUGHTS

CHAPTER 7

REFRAMING TIME-OUT: A CHILL-OUT

Time-outs were a step in the right direction when the idea came out. Arthur Staats coined the term in the '60s, although the practice of putting a child in a corner due to bad behavior had existed before that. Staats had good intentions, and this was his suggestion as an alternative to spanking. And it was a good alternative. Staats stood by his technique and shared, in an article by Vander Schaaf (2019), "Parents are a companion, helper or trainer, and not an authoritarian ruler of the household, using spanking for enforcement and punishment." Vander Schaaf adds, "Some argue it provokes feelings of isolation, abandonment, and anxiety while doing little to teach self-regulation. Others maintain the discipline not only helps a child acquire self-control but also gives parents the opportunity to cool off." Both are true, but it puts the blame on the child; the child needs to cool off. Both parent and child need to cool off and chill out.

Giving everyone a minute to pause, breathe, and take some time to relax and think is what is needed at that moment. However, if you just start yelling, you have lost control over your emotional regulation, and your child sees this and no longer listens to you. At this point, you are not making progress in teaching the child anything, and a pause is needed.

If you feel that you are just someone who is not able to stop those automatic reactions, that is just how you are, this is exactly what must change. It can feel impossible, that there is no space between something happening and your reaction to it, but there is. Using radical awareness, you can become fully present in the moment and then use a mindfulness strategy to decrease your automatic reaction.

1. Explain the Purpose: Explain that you are trying new things to help the family thrive, and one new thing is the chance to chill out when someone is upset. Let your child know that you recognize you could both use a moment to chill out in times like those, and you would like to try it out as a family.

2. Create a Calming Space: Designate a quiet, comfortable place where your child can go to chill out. It can be a cozy corner in their room or a special chair with comforting items like soft toys or blankets. The goal is to create an environment in which they feel safe and calm. And one for you as well, if possible, or go to a private/semiprivate space, as necessary, to continue to ensure the safety of your child.

3. Timing: The recommended length of time is *not* based on age, according to the author; it is based on need. It should be long enough for you and your child to calm down, but not so long that they feel isolated or forget why they're there.

4. Reflection: Once you have both chilled out, have a conversation with your child about what happened. Encourage them to express their feelings and thoughts, discuss better ways they could have handled the situation, and reassure them of your love and support.

An example of reflection using positive language is: "I can see that it can be frustrating for you when I make you feel rushed. I am sorry that I was feeling rushed and then made you feel rushed too. It feels good to chill out and be able to talk to you about it." Another example would be: "I would like to ask if I did or said something that upset you that you can remember from that moment. I was feeling tired, and when you asked me the question, I just yelled without thinking about it, and I am sorry about that. I am not mad at you, and you didn't do anything wrong. I didn't like it when you started yelling in the store, but I can see how you could have been upset, and that was how you were expressing it. Next time, we can find better ways to express our frustration. It doesn't make me not love you. That could never happen."

You may feel that you just don't talk like this, or you can't see yourself talking like this. I would urge you to try it. It may not feel natural at all; however, consider why you aren't able to try and just give it a shot. Being resistant to trying something shows that you are not open to it, and you can change that. It could work. If you feel as if you are sure it won't work before you even try, then your opinion is biased.

Your entire family will benefit from your using positive language in the calmest way possible, as will you. When you become upset and start yelling, you may also notice you start to curse or say mean things. It escalates. Chilling out is necessary and a part of the process of stopping the momentum that leads to spanking and physical discipline.

Taking time to chill out in your daily routine can help to decrease the number of times you need to use this strategy in the moment. Human beings are not designed to thrive with constant activity. We need time to relax, think, daydream, recharge, and process our emotions. Children can become quickly overwhelmed sensorily, and when you are rushing and tired, you may push them beyond their limits and then be upset when they can't handle it emotionally. Or get upset with them when you yourself can't handle it emotionally. Fewer things on your child's schedule will help to allow time for balance and relaxation, which will lead to a less dysregulated child.

ACTIVITY: CHILL-OUT IDEAS

Mutual Chill-Out—When you think of time-out, you think of isolating your child, which can negatively affect them emotionally. A mutual chill-out is possible if you are at home, where you can both be in the same room and do deep breathing together and de-escalate with your child. This isn't always best due to the situation; however, it is helpful to be with your child while they try to process their emotions so that you can assist if needed. Helping them to gain control over their emotions is the intention, so isolating them could make them even more emotional and derail your efforts.

Designing the Space—Part of the fun of this can be talking with your child about what would be helpful for them in their chill-out space. This is something for teens as well, a place they can express their unique personality, if you will let them, and personalize the space so it genuinely brings them comfort and helps them to regain their emotional balance. Try to let them choose items they want; do not direct them to what you think is best. Feeling as if they have a say will increase their desire to use the space.

Watching Something Together—If you are able and have time in the moment, you can watch something funny together. A video that makes you both laugh can help to change the mood and more quickly bring you both back to an emotionally balanced feeling. Ask your child what makes them laugh, and ask them to share it with you. Even if you don't like it, try to move beyond that and enjoy it with them.

Stretching—Our bodies hold on to our unresolved emotions. Sitting and stretching when you are feeling upset can also help to balance out your emotional state. Deep breathing and just lying flat on the floor will help to calm down the nervous system and enable you to calm down.

Listening to Water Sounds—A sound machine in the chill-out area can make a big difference in how quickly you begin to relax. Being emotionally upset and dysregulated is something you are experiencing in your mind as well as your body. You can feel that everything is okay or should be fine, but you still feel shaky; your heart may be racing, or you may be sweating. This is a panic attack and can come on without any observable trigger. The sounds of the water soothe the nervous system.

Cloud Breathing—This is a form of meditation to help you take the thoughts you are having, put them outside of yourself, and attach them to a cloud. Then, watch the cloud and thought float away. As you put your thoughts on the clouds, release your attachment to the thoughts. Let them float away and out of your head. Using guided imagery, you can visualize the clouds and the process of putting the thoughts on the clouds as a way to deepen the relaxation effect.

THINGS TO CONSIDER

- Time-out equals punishment. Chill-out equals relaxation.
- When tensions rise, you and your child need to chill out before interacting further.
- The goal is to regain control over your emotional state, not be punished.

If you find yourself screaming to your child that they need a time-out, you both need a chill-out. When you recognize that your child needs to regroup, check yourself as well, and take time to let the emotion pass and feel more normal again. Then, discussions will be more productive.

You are the one who can change this.
Now is the time to do it.

NOTES AND THOUGHTS

CHAPTER 8

EMOTIONAL INTELLIGENCE: GUIDING CHILDREN'S EMOTIONAL DEVELOPMENT

Beyond disciplinary techniques and behavior management, raising emotionally healthy children involves guiding their emotional development. This chapter introduces the concept of emotional intelligence and provides strategies for nurturing this crucial skill in children.

When we think of intelligence, we typically think of IQ, intellectual intelligence. However, there are multiple types of intelligence; only focusing on one is to overlook your child's individual gifts. Emotional intelligence (EI), a term coined by psychologists Peter Salovey and John D. Mayer, and popularized by psychologist Daniel Goleman, involves the ability to recognize, understand, and manage our own emotions and the emotions of others. It comprises five main components: self-awareness, self-regulation, motivation, empathy, and social skills.

Self-awareness involves recognizing that what you do and say affects others, as well as taking responsibility for the words you use and the energy you are bringing into your interactions with your child and others. When you do not recognize that you are too tired and stressed to have a positive interaction with your child, you will lose your temper and overreact to them. You must gain an awareness of how you are thinking and behaving in order to be able to make changes. Self-regulation involves being able to self-soothe and find ways to regulate your emotions. This is a skill that most adults have not mastered, so please remember that when expecting it from your children; they, too, need to learn and practice.

Motivation—specifically intrinsic motivation that springs from within the person—is fueled by feelings of autonomy, being able to make your own decisions, as well as feelings of competence and relatedness, according to pioneers in the field of motivation, Deci and Ryan (1985). While in my program at the University of Missouri, and early in researching this topic, I created an equation for intrinsic motivation, to give myself another way of looking at it: I + B = IM. Interest plus belief equals intrinsic motivation. If your child isn't interested in something, they are not going to be able to easily motivate themselves to do it, even if they believe they *can* do it. If they *are* interested in something, but don't believe they can do it, they also won't be intrinsically motivated to act.

Empathy is the act of trying to feel what another person is feeling, to better understand their experience. To step into their proverbial shoes, take a few steps, and let yourself feel what the other person is experiencing. When you feel sympathy for someone, you feel sorry for them, and that is nice. However, empathy involves joining the person and sharing in their emotions and processing their feelings, which helps to validate their feelings and allows them to feel heard.

Social skills include using the previously mentioned components in order to have positive interactions with others. For example, when you are consciously being self-aware, you are better able to recognize how you are feeling, if you are upset, and if you need to regulate your emotions. Your being aware of the need is where it starts. Having emotional intelligence is being able to exhibit these characteristics in your daily life and interactions.

You can help to develop your own emotional intelligence and that of your child in multiple ways. One way to do this is to encourage emotional expression. Teach your child that all feelings are valid and that it is okay to express them. Encourage open discussions about feelings, and help your child find the right words to express their emotions.

Another helpful way to increase your child's emotional intelligence is by modeling emotional intelligence in your own behaviors. Show your child what emotional intelligence looks like in action. Manage your own emotions in healthy ways, show empathy towards others, and maintain positive relationships. Your child learns more by observing you and less by what you say.

You can practice emotional regulation by helping your child learn to manage their emotions. Teach them calming techniques like deep breathing, counting to ten, or using positive affirmations. A chill-out will help both of you to get into the mindset of being able to utilize these strategies.

You can help to increase your child's social awareness by encouraging your child to consider others' feelings. This could involve discussing characters' emotions in books or movies, or asking your child how they think their actions might affect others. This will be easier to do if you, too, are a practitioner of these skills. These strategies will help to nurture positive relationships and guide your child in developing healthy relationships. Encourage them to cooperate, share, and resolve conflicts in respectful ways.

Again, it helps if this is what they are living in their home environment. If you tell them to resolve conflicts in a respectful way and then spank them, that doesn't make sense, and they won't trust you.

Children with high emotional intelligence are more likely to have positive social interactions, perform well at school, and have better mental health. They're also less likely to engage in risky behaviors during adolescence. In the long term, adults with high emotional intelligence tend to have successful careers, satisfying relationships, and better overall well-being.

Moreover, guiding your child's emotional development also fosters a deeper parent-child connection. It builds trust and mutual respect, and it equips your child with the emotional tools they'll need to navigate the challenges of life. It's not just about managing behavior; it's about understanding what drives behavior and teaching your child how to manage their emotions in a healthy way.

ACTIVITY: DEVELOPING EMOTIONAL INTELLIGENCE

With your child, discuss the information below and see which of the five components would be helpful in their life and yours.

Seeing a family member sitting alone	Self-awareness, self-regulation, motivation, empathy, and social skills would all be helpful in this situation. With your self-awareness and self-regulation, you won't add negatively to the situation and make it worse unintentionally.
Hearing a family member crying	Again, all of the skills listed will help in this situation. What is motivating your response? Are you triggered by the crying, getting angry, and want it to stop, or are you trying to be empathetic?
Hearing a family member lose it	Self-awareness, self-regulation, empathy, and social skills will help you in this situation. Empathy that this person is upset and unable to control their emotions can help you to see them as struggling and in need of help, instead of needing someone to yell and tell them to stop.
Feeling as if you want to cry	Showing yourself empathy is a way to help develop it and have it come more naturally towards others as well.

THINGS TO CONSIDER

- Emotional intelligence refers to the ability to understand and take responsibility for your own emotions and actions.
- Increasing your emotional intelligence can be done by becoming more self-aware and using mindfulness strategies like deep breathing and journaling.
- You will be better able to teach your child how to increase their emotional intelligence if you have already worked on increasing your own.

An emotionally intelligent parent recognizes that their child is their own person with their own feelings, wants, and needs. When your child sees that you are able to control your own emotional state, they can model that and learn how to do it.

You are the one who can change this.
Now is the time to do it.

NOTES AND THOUGHTS

CHAPTER 9

THE FIVE-STEP PLAN: PAUSE/ BREATHE/ASK/LISTEN/REFRAME

This is your five-step plan for making the change from spanking to not spanking. Put a bookmark on this page to refer back to when you are in the moment and trying to make this change. It can take months of daily practice to develop a new unconscious habit, so don't give up too soon. This may not be natural for you, so recognize that; do not let that interfere with your progress. You can do this; it just takes the ability to stop your automatic reaction and make a new choice.

PAUSE—The first step is to pause. This involves stopping your automatic reaction using radical awareness. When you feel yourself about to say something or blow up, STOP. Stop yourself right then. You are in control of what you think, do, and say. Being heightened emotionally and really upset does not mean you have to give up control and repeat the automatic reaction. An automatic reaction is not a conscious thought; when you react automatically, you are not present in the moment. That is why radical awareness is needed to interrupt your usual patterns and put an even wider gap between the situation and your reaction to it.

BREATHE—The next step is to breathe. This may sound simplistic, but it is critical in decreasing your stress level so that you can stop yourself from hitting your child. You are creating a new reaction to being annoyed. Pause and then immediately breathe deeply; that is how you regain your power. You do not think clearly when you are upset; you react in unintended and heightened ways when you are not thinking clearly. Breathing deeply and with focus will help you immensely in this moment.

ASK—After you have relaxed a bit and have stopped the automatic reaction, ask your child how they are feeling and what is going on with them. You can assume they are misbehaving intentionally; however, when they are losing it, that may not be the reason. They may not feel well; they may be hungry, tired, upset, etc. So asking is important; you want them to have the opportunity to be heard, validated, and taken seriously.

LISTEN—After you ask, you must actively listen to their response. This means you listen with conscious awareness and the intention of understanding, not responding or lecturing. Actively listen and share what you hear; they may say what you heard was not what they meant and then attempt to explain their feelings again. You must again listen with the intention of understanding, not responding. This may take a minute; being patient throughout this process is critical. You are showing your child that you do indeed care about what they are saying about their feelings; you genuinely care and are not trying to rush them.

REFRAME—After you've listened and your child feels heard, you reframe how you see the original situation. Reframing is a strategy developed by Dr. Aaron Beck, who is credited as the father of cognitive behavior therapy, or CBT. The Beck Institute website reports that "depressed patients often experienced negative thoughts about themselves, the world, and/or the future. These thoughts, or cognitions, appeared to occur spontaneously, and Dr. Beck referred to them as automatic thoughts." His idea is that thoughts, feelings, and behaviors are interconnected. His method was to have the patients first identify and then evaluate their automatic thoughts and recognize the distortions in their thinking. And with this recognition, be able to make change. This leads to the realization that you have a patterned way of explaining things to yourself and that your immediate reactions could be pessimistic. Your instinct is to expect the worst or some other negative outcome, and to assume that you are correct and act accordingly.

For example, you could interpret your child's failure to respond as a lack of respect and have an automatic reaction similar to "You need to listen to me when I talk to you; you are being disrespectful." Steps one and two—pausing and breathing—stop your automatic reaction. Then, ask your child how they are feeling and listen actively. This may mean you need to stop what you are doing and give them your full attention. If you are not really listening, they will be able to tell, so they may not trust your responses. After you listen to your child, repeat back what you understood them to say and ensure it is correct. Rushing them when they are trying to express themselves and having difficulties will discourage them from sharing with you in the future.

After going through the five steps, if you are still having difficulties, start the process all over again. You may need to chill out more before you are ready to really listen. It is highly unlikely that you will still have the impulse to spank them after completing the process. It is the automatic reaction from frustration that leads to the physical means of discipline. Stopping that will enable you to feel hopeful that you can do this.

The more you are able to stop your automatic reaction and give your conscious attention to regaining your cool, the easier and more natural it will become. After completing the process, you will have gained a deeper understanding of what your child is experiencing emotionally. This can lead to increased empathy and the desire to share unconditional love with them, not physical punishment.

ACTIVITY: PRACTICING THE PROCESS

Situation One—Screaming in Public

1. **Pause**—Don't worry about other people or what they think. I know that can be easier said than done, but you are trying a better way; the understanding of strangers is not important. Take a moment to pause and stop the automatic reaction.
2. **Breathe**—Until your heightened emotions calm, breathe in through your nose and out through your mouth.
3. **Ask**—Respectfully ask your child what they are feeling. Grabbing them by the arm and physically restraining them is not going to be helpful as you do this. Forcibly controlling their body will add to their distress; it won't help.
4. **Listen**—This requires you to have done deep breathing, so if you are having trouble actively listening, do more breathing. Repeat back to your child what you think they mean, and confirm you are correct. Repeat this process until your child feels you understand how they are feeling.
5. **Reframe**—Reconsider how you are interpreting the situation and find a nonphysical way to help your child manage their emotions as you manage your own.

Situation Two—Having a Tantrum and Crying at Home

1. **Pause**—Pause and stop your automatic reaction. Both of you go to your chill-out spots.
2. **Breathe**—Breathe in through your nose and out through your mouth for a few minutes. Lie down if you can; really relax.
3. **Ask**—When you are feeling composed, respectfully ask your child what they are feeling. If they are still having a tantrum, let them know you would like to talk to them when they feel ready. If they are crying but not having a tantrum, you can ask if you can get them something like water or a cold or warm washcloth.

4. **Listen**—Practice active listening, and repeat back what you think they mean; confirm it is correct. Give them time to collect their thoughts; they do not process information the same way you do. Repeat this step until your child feels understood.
5. **Reframe**—Reconsider how you are interpreting the situation, and find a nonphysical way to help your child manage their emotions as you process your own.

THINGS TO CONSIDER

- The practice of spanking is a habit that you've learned over time; you can change it with radical awareness.
- It takes daily practice for a minimum of a month to make these new methods into habits.
- When you lose your cool—and everyone does at times—start the five-step process again; you may need to pause and breathe for a while before you are ready to move on.

This five-step process is something you can use not only with your child, but at work, in social situations, and out with strangers in public to help you have more positive and meaningful interactions.

You are the one who can change this.
Now is the time to do it.

NOTES AND THOUGHTS

CHAPTER 10

REAL-LIFE EXAMPLES: SUCCESS STORIES OF NONPHYSICAL DISCIPLINE

These stories are being shared to help provide examples of how this change can look in your life and with your family. Identities have been changed to ensure anonymity. You may be able to see yourself in these situations, which will help you to effectively implement change in your life and family.

As a marriage and family therapist, I have the privilege of helping families successfully navigate this journey, which includes hearing stories about how they get around difficulties and stick with their new approach. I feel hearing these stories will help you as well. I send my appreciation to everyone I work with for their dedication to this mission.

FAMILY STORY: ANXIETY AND PAST TRAUMA

During their childhood, most people experience some sort of trauma that can affect how they later parent when they are triggered and anxious. The mother in this story is divorced and has a five-year-old child; the mother experienced emotional trauma that began around the same age. Her desire to be a good mother was at the root of much of her current anxiety, and this same desire triggered her and took her back to traumatic memories with her own mother, so her lens was clouded during interactions with her child. When her child doesn't listen as intently or quickly as she'd like, she becomes overanxious, her tone becomes harsher, and she raises her voice, which the child interprets as anger because of them. From the child's perspective, they don't understand what they did wrong, so they act out in a variety of ways, including crying hysterically.

Now, the woman, whose base intention is to be a good mother, is becoming even more heightened emotionally and reaching panic levels. She has learned to notice sooner when her child is becoming dysregulated and upset. She reports seeing some of those red flags and ignoring them due to being in a hurry to get things done.

Stopping this one practice of ignoring the warning signs enabled her to practice the five steps before she was too upset to do so. And once she mastered that step, hearing her child was easier, and she was able to have more patience in actively listening and truly validating her child. Her child benefitted immensely from the focused attention, and it seemed that was the child's primary need.

Before learning and practicing the five-step approach, this mother had viewed her child's need for attention as too much and unnecessary. She didn't validate her child's needs. Her assumption that her child "just wanted attention" prevented her from recognizing they really did need more focused attention from her, and from acknowledging that the child wasn't asking for too much. This stemmed from her childhood trauma. As a child, she was told that her needs for attention were too much; her needs were not valued. Not receiving attention can make you feel that you are not valuable, that your needs are not real, and that you don't deserve what you need.

Now that this mother and child are experienced in the five-step process, they do it naturally. The mother reports that because of their genuine mutual respect now, she can't believe she ever spanked her child to begin with. It's working for them, and her child is getting along better in school and enjoys describing their emotions. Working the steps has also helped the mother to disconnect from the emotional ties to her past, which no longer serve or support her, and to be more present with her child.

FAMILY STORY: BLENDED FAMILY FROM DIFFERENT CULTURES

Each culture views physical discipline differently; different ideas and approaches can exist within a blended family. This family consists of a mother who has two children from a previous marriage and one child with her current husband. The father also has two children from a previous marriage, and they have all of the kids together on weekends. The mother's family of origin was very open with affection and did not spank; the father's family of origin was not open at all with affection; they spanked and used other objects to deliver physical punishments to show the children who was in charge. Even though the father reports being "beaten" at times, he still feels that spanking is something he wants to perpetuate. The mother is horrified by this and has difficulty understanding why he would want to do this thing that is terrible and something he himself had to endure.

The father explained that this is how disciplining was done in his family, and he feels it helps the children to listen and behave. Despite the parents not agreeing on how to manage the kids' behavior, the father continued to spank. One night, one of the kids told him they hated him and ran out of the room. When this happened, it led to more spanking and heightened tensions.

As Dad began to reframe his own behaviors and reactions, he started to see things differently, and that enabled him to agree to try the process. As he began to chill out with his children more, he recognized that they had things to say; they were trying to be heard. His upbringing had caused him to believe that children should be seen and not heard. It is still a work in progress for them, but due to the father's willingness to look at things differently, and pause and breathe as long as needed, he no longer resorts to spanking and continues to find new ways that work for them and the children.

ACTIVITY: YOUR NEW STORY

Think about and visualize what you would like your family dynamic to be. Imagine having interactive and fun conversations with your kids. See yourself having these interactions, and examine how they make you feel. Think through and reflect on how you will make these changes and how you will begin to stop your automatic reactions. Writing down your thoughts allows your brain to process the information from a different perspective, which can deepen your understanding.

THINGS TO CONSIDER

- This is something you can do, and you are the author of your story.
- You can practice the strategies shared in this book and make positive changes in your life, your children's lives, and your family dynamics.
- Talking and sharing with friends is a helpful way to help strengthen these practices.

When you become more confident in stopping your automatic reaction and using the five-step process, you will be a model for friends who are struggling with these same issues.

You are the one who can change this.
Now is the time to do it.

NOTES AND THOUGHTS

CHAPTER 11

A THERAPIST'S ROLE: SUPPORTING PARENTS IN THIS TRANSITION

Making these changes may be easier than you imagine right now. One thing that will help you be successful in making changes is to seek the services of a mental health professional. There are multiple types of therapists. I am an LMFT, a licensed marriage and family therapist, and I use a systems-based approach. You are part of a family system, and each individual part affects the other parts, which prevents any individual within it from being singled out as the problem. Every family member contributes to what is happening within the family system.

For some people, it does not feel natural to talk about personal issues with someone outside of their family. That is perfectly understandable, and without experience in working with a therapist, you may think that is always the case. As a therapist, I have taken an oath to, first, do no harm. I have worked at clearing my own biases and being able to hold an unconditional, positive regard for all of my clients. In session, they have a safe space to explore difficult topics in a safe, therapeutic space. The profession is monitored, regulated, and most therapists have something to offer; it is a safe place for you to try.

You may find that you would benefit from individual therapy in addition to the family sessions. If you have experienced your own trauma and are being triggered in these situations, processing your past issues will enable you to succeed in achieving radical awareness and stopping your automatic reactions. A professional therapist does not have any stake in your situation; because they begin as strangers, they are able to offer objective feedback. You do not have to agree with everything the therapist says; however, you deserve the chance to thrive and to receive the unconditional support a professional therapist can give.

Take the time to consult with a therapist and ensure that you feel comfortable talking with them. Creating a therapeutic bond is critical to reaching the core of your issues and making lasting change. The five-step process offered here does not take that long; however, learning to stop being triggered into an automatic response takes time. As you try the process again and again each day, sharing your progress with the therapist will allow them to see it in a larger context and hopefully to offer helpful suggestions on how to perform each of the steps as intended. They will help you stay accountable, to keep your lens clear so that you can hear your family more clearly, and to prevent the situation from becoming worse.

Reach out through your insurance provider to look for therapists that are in your network, or if you are paying with cash, seek a therapist in your price range. It can be frustrating to find a therapist you hit it off with and then find out you can't see them. After a few of these experiences, you will be ready to give up. Good therapists exist; they will be able to see what you are trying to accomplish with the five-step strategy offered here, and they will help you succeed. And if you do not feel it is working out with a therapist, try a new one. This is your life, these are your sessions, and you should feel as if you are being genuinely supported and led by a professional.

ACTIVITY: PATH TO CHANGE

Take a minute to put your plan on paper; make a list of things to do to keep you on track to finding a therapist to help you implement these changes. Below are a few suggestions to get you started and spaces provided for notes.

Through your insurance provider, research approved providers.

___

___

___

Think through—and discuss with your partner, if applicable—your plan to start therapy and find ways to avoid using physical means of discipline. Try to get on the same page, even if just with yourself.

___

___

___

List of pros and cons for seeing a therapist.

Pros	Cons

Time frame when you would like to get started:

___

Questions you have for the therapist:

___

___

___

___

THINGS TO CONSIDER

- Talking with a licensed marriage and family therapist will help everyone in the family better understand these strategies.
- A therapist can provide a safe, nonjudgmental environment in which to help everyone in the family honestly address their role in the family dynamics.
- Individual, couple, and family therapy sessions can help you to make personal changes that help each member of your family to thrive.

Therapy can be strange if you haven't done it before; however, a qualified therapist can help you to look at yourself and the situation from alternative perspectives, which will allow you to make lasting changes and will support you throughout this process.

You are the one who can change this.
Now is the time to do it.

NOTES AND THOUGHTS

CHAPTER 12

A BRIGHTER FUTURE: RAISING EMOTIONALLY HEALTHY CHILDREN

The benefits from the strategies shared in this book go beyond stopping the toxic practice of spanking; these methods are meant to help you change how you think about your role as a parent. If we didn't get to experience the childhood we imagined or hoped for, and if we were spanked, hit, slapped, whipped, beaten or made to feel less than, but still feel we have managed okay, we see no urgency in making a change, or even the necessity for it. However, just because you have been able to manage doesn't mean it was best for you or that you are thriving as well as you could be. You overcame it, thankfully, to the degree that you have, but it isn't lifting you up and helping you to thrive.

You have good intentions and a desire to parent well, or you wouldn't have picked up this book. Your child or children deserve the best start in life they can have. And you deserve to reach your potential as a parent and to be able to give your children, and yourself, the gift of unconditional love.

Some people think that emotional intelligence comes naturally and that you don't have to teach it, or that it is taught in school, but it isn't. There are activities that foster emotional intelligence, but it needs to be taught and reinforced in the home environment for it to really sink in. Children can be told by their teacher that they should try to be emotionally intelligent and feel empathy for others; however, if they go home and are not shown any empathy or compassion, they will feel confused and frustrated.

This emotionally healthy childhood you wish to create for your children is well worth your time and effort. You have the opportunity to break generational bonds of physical disciplining, to abolish the mindset that you are the parent, they are the child, and you know best. Each individual person knows, from within, what is best. You may feel as if you know what is best for your child, but in reality, what you know is what you *want* for them, what you *think* is best. A child hears the beat of their own drummer, and if we're not careful, we can extinguish that sound.

So many adults I meet still do not know their purpose or passion when they are nearing forty years old. You know what it is when you are young—you just know it and can feel it. You probably shared your childhood dreams and your own unique thinking with someone. If you were shut down, cut off, silenced, or told you needed too much attention, you can empathize with your child whom you want never to feel that way.

I know you are exhausted. You work hard and most likely need more support, as most people do. Making new friends who are also implementing this change will be so helpful to you. This effort you are making is worth it; it is something you will look back on as a changing moment for you and your family.

When a child feels emotionally supported and safe to express unwanted behaviors without fear of not being loved, they can learn and move towards their potential. As this happens, you will also grow, feel increased happiness in your life, and experience a stronger bond with your child and family.

How you are handling this now is laying the groundwork for your child's future automatic reactions. You can set them up for success by teaching and practicing mindfulness strategies with them daily. This will help them to automatically pause, breathe—without it feeling unnatural—and intentionally react with increasing levels of conscious awareness as they mature.

Keep up the good work, and reach out to me if I can help in any way! I would love to hear your personal stories. I wish you much success.

ACTIVITY: NOTICING THE CHANGES, BE IN A STATE OF GRATITUDE

What you focus on grows. When you pay attention to positive changes your children and you are making, it will motivate you to keep trying.

Use this page to make notes of positive changes you are seeing in your child or children, in your family system, and in yourself.

THINGS TO CONSIDER

- Your child is their own individual person with their own dreams and life path.
- You want your child to be excited about their own life and know that they have your unconditional love and support.
- Your role as a parent is not about disciplining; it is about teaching.

You will experience true joy when you see your child learn and feel confident, even when making mistakes and trying again. You can bring comfort, safety, and understanding to your child who is still trying to make sense of the world. They will grow and develop in positive ways you couldn't have imagined.

You are the one who can change this.
Now is the time to do it.

NOTES AND THOUGHTS

THANK YOU

Thank you for taking the time to read this book and for challenging yourself to stop physically disciplining your child. I see you and validate you for trying something new; that isn't easy. Also, to challenge long-held beliefs is not something we do often; it isn't necessarily fun. You can look your children in the eye, apologize for what has happened up to this point, and promise to try to do better. Making this change will create positive ripple effects in your life and within your family system, the benefits of which you can't even imagine at this moment.

Give yourself time to practice the process; it takes as long as it takes. You will still lose your cool sometimes and yell, but every time you don't cross over into physical discipline, that is a win. Keep trying, and you will eventually be able to stop yelling. Once we start shouting, they stop listening.

You may find that you would benefit from some individual therapy, as well, to provide you with a space to talk about more personal issues. You can do this, and if you are willing to take the time, you will be successful. Please let me know if I can be of further assistance.

REFERENCES

Afifi, T. O., Mota, N. P., Dasiewicz, P., MacMillan, H. L., and Sareen, J. (2012), "Physical punishment and mental disorders: Results from a nationally representative US sample," *Pediatrics, 130*(2), 184–192, https://doi.org/10.1542/peds.2011-2947.

Buchanan, G. M., and Seligman, M. E. (1995), *Explanatory style*, Psychology Press.

Chase, N. (1999), "Burdened children: Theory, research, and treatment of Parentification," https://doi.org/10.4135/9781452220604.

Gershoff, E. T. (2002), "Corporal punishment by parents and associated child behaviors and experiences: A meta-analytic and theoretical review," *Psychological Bulletin*, *128*(4), 539-579, https://doi.org/10.1037/0033-2909.128.4.539.

Greenberg, R., and Jurkovic, G. J. (1999), "Lost childhoods: The plight of the parentified child," *Family Relations*, *48*(1), 101, https://doi.org/10.2307/585689.

Grogan-Kaylor, A. (2005), "Corporal punishment and the growth trajectory of children's antisocial behavior," *Child Maltreatment*, *10*(3), 283-292, https://doi.org/10.1177/1077559505277803.

Lansford, J. E., Wager, L. B., Bates, J. E., Pettit, G. S., and Dodge, K. A. (2012), "Forms of spanking and children's externalizing behaviors," *Family Relations*, *61*(2), 224-236, https://doi.org/10.1111/j.1741-3729.2011.00700.x.

Lipton, B. H. (2015), "The biology of belief: Unleashing the power of consciousness, matter and miracles,"

MacKenzie, M. J., Nicklas, E., Waldfogel, J., and Brooks-Gunn, J. (2011), "Corporal punishment and child behavioural and cognitive outcomes through 5 years of age: Evidence from a contemporary urban birth cohort study," *Infant and Child Development*, *21*(1), 3-33, https://doi.org/10.1002/icd.758.

Peterson, C., Maier, S. F., and Seligman, M. E. (1993), *Learned helplessness: A theory for the age of personal control*. Oxford University Press, USA.

Rosyada, A., and Retnomurti, A. B. (2017), "The use of positive language on children education to build children's positive behaviour," *Scope : Journal of English Language Teaching*, *1*(01), 1, https://doi.org/10.30998/scope.v1i01.868.

Vander Shaaf, S. (2019), "Ever wondered who invented the time-out?" heraldtribune.com, https://www.heraldtribune.com/story/lifestyle/health-fitness/2019/04/02/ever-wonder-who-invented-timeout/5558423007/.

APPENDIX A

MINDFULNESS STRATEGIES

Deep Breathing—Focus on taking a deep breath in through your nose and out through your mouth. Close your eyes if that helps you to relax, or you can do it while working or engaged in a conversation, if needed. Take a few—three is good, most times—to help you relax and to decrease your heightened reaction. This is a simple yet very powerful tool that you will use daily to help you manage your frustrations, as that is typically where spanking comes in.

Cloud Meditation—Sit comfortably with your eyes open or closed, whichever you prefer. As thoughts come into your mind, without judgment, remove them from your mind. Using visualization, attach the thoughts to a cloud, and then watch it float away. Don't be threatened by your thoughts; lovingly place them on the cloud, and send them on their way.

Five-Senses Strategy—Focusing on one thing in your environment that is associated with each of your senses will help ground you, which can decrease anxiety. For example, focus on something you can smell, something you can taste, something you can feel, something you can see, and something you can hear. Focusing on these elements in your present environment will help to distract your thoughts from something that could be triggering an old memory and making it more difficult to be present in the moment.

Grounding Strategy—Sit or stand, and imagine steel rods—or roots, whichever you prefer—extending out of the bottoms of your feet and buried deep in the floor. Let yourself feel being grounded and safely secured to the earth. This can help to decrease anxiety and ease feelings of dissociation that can come up when you reach a level of frustration at which you could spank.

Guided Imagery—In your mind's eye, visualize an image that brings you peace, feelings of joy, or a smile to your face. This is helpful when you are repeatedly thinking about something unwanted. Replace the image with one of your choice that you enjoy; this will help decrease negative feelings.

Observer Perspective—Imagine that you are stepping outside of your body and hovering around the ceiling of your room. See the situation as the observer, removed from being so present consciously in the interaction. This can help you to step outside of yourself to see how your automatic reaction looks from that perspective. It will help you to remove your emotional attachment to the situation and see it as if it is happening to someone else, which provides a helpful, new perspective.

Radical Awareness—Becoming radically aware in any given moment helps you use your conscious awareness to be more present and to stop automatic reactions.

Starfish Strategy—Gently and slowly, trace the outside of your hand with the pointer finger of your other hand, outlining the edges. This creates a strange sensation that helps to draw your focus to the sensation and away from the emotional trigger so that you can relax and recenter your emotional self.

NOTE: Please check the web for many more helpful mindfulness strategies you can try.

ACKNOWLEDGMENTS

This book would not have been possible without the support and encouragement of many people. First and foremost, I would like to thank my publisher, Lisa Umina, the president of Halo Publishing, who believed in this project from the very beginning and guided me through the publishing process. Also, thank you to my editor, Camila del Aguila, for her keen insights and tireless efforts in refining my manuscript. I am also deeply grateful to Fernanda Ramirez with Halo Publishing for her efforts on this book.

I am indebted to Dr. Janelle Barlow for her invaluable expertise and for assisting me in having the knowledge and courage to write my first book.

My deepest gratitude goes to my family, especially my spouse, Richard, who supported me unconditionally and provided endless support in every way. To my wonderful children, Brandon and Logan, thank you for your constant encouragement and for listening to my endless musings about the book.

Lastly, I wish to thank you, the reader, for your interest in this book. Any errors or omissions are mine alone.

JULIE ROBINSON, PSYD, LMFT, M.ED.

LET'S CONNECT

Website:
www.lvtherapycenter.com

Facebook:
https://www.facebook.com/lvtherapycenter/

Youtube:
https://www.youtube.com/@lasvegastherapycenter

Email:
julie@lvtherapycenter.com

www.ingramcontent.com/pod-product-compliance
Lightning Source LLC
Chambersburg PA
CBHW060807110426
42739CB00032BA/3127
* 9 7 8 1 6 3 7 6 5 6 6 1 7 *